WHEN WE WERE WATER

Praise for Raúl Sánchez's Previous Collections

When There Were No Borders

Sánchez writes borderless in borderless times. He breaks through the ancient Mexica figure of death and transformation, Coatlicue, to poems as pyramids, to the Sea of the Salish in the Pacific Northwest and on to cool-rebel Pachuco dialect of the US-Mexico borderlands. He cooks on a rotating rainbow-colored pan, he spices, he refuses to present his "papers" at the border stop. There are nectars, harvests, the always-farmworker fields, a detention center to tend to with resources and a poet. Open this collection—hold on, there is a "pirinola," an ever-spinning umbrella-shaped candy with a pointed tip burning colors, lights and stories that will take you to Latinx multi-dimensional magic. A precise, moving mural, this text of visitations of "life, precious life!" Sánchez's delights as he writes, as he tears across those borderlines, dancing. Magnificent poetics to take home and to take you out.

—Juan Felipe Herrera, Poet Laureate of the United States Emeritus

All Our Brown-Skinned Angels

Mexican American Raúl Sánchez raises his poetic voice in languages twice removed from the indigenous language of his ancestors, but with well more than double the fervor. Language is embodied in the essence of personal and political struggle, as evidenced in these lines from the poem "My Father Was a Bracero": "He didn't want me to live / by my strong back, strong arms / but by my words." This ardent inaugural collection by Sánchez is filled with poems of identity—cultural, familial and personal. *All Our Brown-Skinned Angels* is part civil protest, part personal celebration, completely impassioned.

—Lana Hechtman Ayers, author of *The Autobiography of Rain*

WHEN WE WERE WATER

New & Selected Poems

Raúl Sánchez

World Enough
Writers

Published in the United States of America by
World Enough Writers

Copyright © 2026 by Raúl Sánchez

All rights reserved. Except for the inclusion of brief quotations within a review, no part of this book may be reproduced or transmitted in any form or by any means, electronic or mechanical, including photocopying, recording, or any information or retrieval system, without permission in writing from the editor/publisher and/or copyright holder of a particular work. Please note: anyone wishing to reproduce or republish a poem from this anthology should contact the poet and/or copyright holder of the poem.

ISBN: 978-1-937797-11-9

Cover art: *Sedona*, oil on canvas, 2001, by Alfredo Arreguín

Author photo by Carlos Rodriguez

Book Design by Tonya Namura using Minion Pro

World Enough Writers, an imprint of Concrete Wolf, publishes
poetry collections and anthologies of
global importance and interest.

For information, please contact the publisher:

World Enough Writers
c/o Concrete Wolf
PO Box 2220
Newport, OR 97365-0163

Email: WorldEnoughWriters@gmail.com
Website: https://worldenoughwriters.com

*For all the immigrant youth
 and all the Brown-Skinned Angels*

*let your poems be Earth prayers tearing down barriers,
feet grounded, and yet, ethereal, like radio poems*
—Francisco X. Alarcón, "Radio Poems"

Table of Contents

I Poems from *All Our Brown-Skinned Angels*

Gravity	5
Minimum Wage	6
Brown Angels at Work	7
Mexico City in Dalí's Eyes	9
Fernando	10
In Praise of Poets Responding to SB 1070	11
Right Time, Wrong Place	12
Where I'm From	14
MEX – I – CAN	15
All Our Brown-Skinned Angels	17
Cliff's Edge	19
Dandelion	20
Flower Girl	21
Ten Years Gone	22
My Father Was a Bracero	23

II Poems from *When There Were No Borders*

Itlapaltin nemiliztli	27
Colores de la vida	28
Colors of Life	29
Mexica Tiahui	30
Cintéotl	31
My Tongue / Mi lengua	32
Smoke	33
Milagros	35
1960	37
Show Me Your Papers	39
Cuando no había fronteras / When There Were No Borders	41
Life / Vida	42
Nationalization	43
Wind	44
Sanctuary	45

Your Body	47
Three Words	49
Poets' Temple	50
Excuse Me Absent Poet But…	52
Selecting a Reader	53
A New Star in the Darkened Sky	54
Reminiscing	56
Borinquen	58
Found Sonnets	60
My Experience at the Detention Center and Why I Became Interested in Mentoring the Youth in Detention	61
National Poem in Your Pocket Day	63
Kubota Garden, Seattle	64
Ode to an Oak Tree	65
Oda a un roble viejo	66
Greensward	67
Césped	68
before I'm gone	70

III New Poems: *When We Were Water*

Art Is Life	73
Bean Around the Globe	74
Whisper	76
Guatemalan Miracle	77
Daffodils and Dandelions	79
Washing the Dishes	80
Monk's Dream on Monet's *Nymphéas bleus*	81
Only a Dream	82
We Danced	83
Visit to Dachau	84
Today I Killed a Spider—Accidentally	86
By the line of the spine	88
Crack the Pot	89
Dear Papi	90
Dissolved	91

Essential Heroes	93
February Snow	95
For Don Victor Sánchez	96
I Miss the Rain	97
I Met a Brown-Skinned Angel	98
I Want to Worship	100
In Memory of Uncle Manuel	101
In the Water	102
Inantzin / Madre / Mother	103
India Flashback	105
Mother's Garden	107
Ode to an Old Typewriter	108
Our Lives Suspended Until Further Notice	109
Potato Revenge	110
Remember When We Were Water?	111
Second Chance	112
The Man on the Exit Ramp	113
Travelling by Whale	114
Two Palm Trees	115
Vanished	116
What Work Is	117
Why Poetry?	118
Notes	119
Acknowledgments	121
Gratitude	123
About the Artist	125
About the Author	127

WHEN WE WERE WATER

I
Poems from
All Our Brown-Skinned Angels

*Poets are the unacknowledged legislators
of the world.*

—Percy Bysshe Shelley, *A Defence of Poetry
and Other Essays*

Gravity

A woman next to me asks
are you writing a poem?
Scribbles I say
from all the places
I left behind:
family mysteries
incidents come to mind
toilet paper ripping beyond the notches
social arts delivered on snack trays
my father's business
Uncle Parcel's tips challenged
revenge's mastery
philosophers' teachings
unfamiliar sand tricks
seventy-five degrees longitude
being submerged in holy rivers
anointed "paramahamsas"
above the self, my self
not for herself, itself
half-empty whiskey glasses
translated stories five degrees below
the tropic of cancer
scorching sand illuminated
reflecting sunglasses
empty whiskey glasses
no faith in things unknown
findable frequencies of facts
the world a glass full of rain
the world a plane
landing on a tiny runway
the world at my feet
held down by gravity

Minimum Wage

He risked
climbing walls
jumping barbed wire
crossing deserts, mountains
crawling sewage ducts
eluding *la migra*

He almost died, but survived
and made it to the promised
land

He works—
dishwashing
table serving
housecleaning
dog walking
car washing
yard working
housekeeping

This is his work
his community
his church
his neighborhood
his family
his home

Yet there are border wars
laws that make migrants outlaws

He does what others don't like
He risks his life every day
for the minimum

Brown Angels at Work

Brown angels are everywhere
We observe them mowing lawns
raking, blowing leaves
dangling from tall buildings

washing windows, painting
roofing houses
They are in your kitchens
serving, smiling

They park your cars
Out in all kinds of weather watch
them picking fruits and vegetables
breaking their backs

On freeway ramps we witness them
selling flowers, cherries, and strawberries
Brown angels are attending church
going to night school, college-bound

These angels don't fly
They walk the same sun-baked
earth that you and I do
sowing seeds

of prosperity deep down
in this American soil
This economy's wheels turn
on the axles of immigrant sweat

brown angel sweat
Lately the wheels are stuck
in intimidation's mud
discrimination's muck

If brown angels could fly
hover over fertile fields and cities
of *this* American land they would
perform miracles, *Milagros*!

Mexico City in Dalí's Eyes

unfinished stucco houses
brick-and-mortar narrow doors
exposed rebar scratching the sky
winding cobblestone streets
too many cars, buses
changing lanes with no warning
pedestrian crossing traffic lanes
suicidal clowns, windshield washers
stoplight vendors
traffic cops, corrupt cops
prostitutes, cathedral bells, bars,
taco stands, street beggars,
sidewalk vendors' plastic shoes
melting asphalt,
jarras dripping *pulque*
dogs on rooftops barking to the wind

Fernando

His voice a squawky reed
telling long-gone stories
of his town
lost in the past

Fernando talks about bridges
and rivers crossed,
leaving behind his verdant village
where everybody knew each other's
joy and pain

"Hace mucho frío"
It's too cold here
he mutters into the sound
of the rake and the rustling leaves

Fernando keeps hoping
to wake up in the America
balmy as his passionate dreams
the America others foretold

In Praise of Poets Responding to SB 1070

Behind the great wooden gate
past the threshold
our memories blossom in the open air
under the blue star-spangled sky

Our cultures coalesce
into a tapestry of colors and accents
and flavors—café con leche
black and white

Cuba, México, Venezuela, Colombia
Borinquen bella escuchen mi llanto
la patria aquella que se ve de lejos
y se siente cerca

Argentina, Chile, Paraguay
far away yet near, our thoughts
y pensamientos connect
place with state of mind

Our traditions link families
create lasting friendships
Our traditions strengthen bonds
Our voices rise

poets, writers, artists
aligned with ethnic pride
with dignity and respect
love for *la Raza*

We are just another shade of brown
living en el norte, north of Aztlán
United in this land
we are all free Americans

Right Time, Wrong Place

"You have the right to remain silent"
First time I heard the bark
was after being slammed
up against a police car
corner of 5th and Main
trigger-trained, baton-wielding
black uniforms with covered badges
next to the chicken stand
The corner street lamplight
could bear no witness

*"Anything you say can and will
be used against you in a court of law"*
Baton pokes in my sides my ribs

"Spread your legs now!"
Hands up against the door
steel cuffs pinched tight
intimidating rage blasted at me
not knowing what to say
I didn't say anything—
they made me *"respond"*

"You have the right to an attorney"
Only if I knew what to do
I couldn't choose an attorney
nor the drunks, prostitutes
transsexuals, petty thieves
booked into the precinct like me
fingerprinted, strip-searched
latex finger probing private cavity
found nothing—only stench

"*If you cannot afford an attorney
one will be provided for you*"
Benevolence: assigned public defender
who recommends I plead "*guilty*"
All they found on me—
a box-cutting knife
concealed "*weapon*" they said
two-year probation
"*lucky*" it is just a misdemeanor
not a felony
my attorney said

"*Do you understand the rights
I have just read to you?*"
Of course not
I've never been arrested
Could you repeat that Mr. Officer?
Who's that Miranda guy?
There are no rights on the street—
scare tactics, harsh words
I submitted to it
If I resisted I could've had my head
slammed on concrete

"*With these rights in mind
do you wish to speak to me?*"
Told the cops I didn't have anything
They pounded me with questions
determined to get me
for something, anything, because
"*I looked like the guy they were after*"

They inked my fingers black
booked me
with equal injustice for all

Where I'm From

after George Ella Lyon

I am from *cazuelas de barro*
from *mole* and tamales
I am from the restaurant my father owned
My burning mouth remembers
I am from the honeysuckle creeper
the fig tree, jacaranda
whose long-gone limbs I remember
as if they were my own
I am from fiestas and piñatas
from late nights and early mornings
from *chocolate caliente*
I am from *apúrate y callate*
from *Reyes Magos y dulces*
I'm from Victor and Elena
and *más vale tarde que nunca*
I'm from México, *barrio norte*
caldo de hongos
from *paso del norte*
to work the fields
good times, from *familia*
From mother's closet stash
of letters sent and received
her hand-embroidered *I Love You*'s
I am from learning English in my youth
from hard work
from love
still growing along my family tree

MEX – I – CAN

Be all you can be, "*Ese*"!
Shiny shoes, baggy pants, buttoned-up shirt
bandana on my head, standing on the corner
Looking   watching   thinking…

Brown skin,
"*Familia*" mixed blood
Mestizo, Chicano, Latino
"*Mi tierra*," here, there
Over there…

We are here, we have been here,
We're not going anywhere, "*Ese*"!

"*La línea*," jumping, running
towards the *Promised Land*
wet brow, sweat, the hard labor
of dignity and pride

When we work the land
sun, rain, fertile thoughts of freedom
To live, to love, to grow
Cruising life "*bajito y suavecito*"
taking the bumps slooooow and easy

My "*familia*" migrated north before
borders and chain-link fences
feelings, political defenses
green cards, racial profiles
"*Mi familia*" severed…

"*México lindo, Sacramento adorado
En Tejas te dejo mi corazón mojado*"
A river runs through

drowning…
our hopes "*y su esperanza*"

American dream, impossible dream
Label me not for I won't
live on dreaming
Stereotyped "in the box"
shut out by prejudice

I am, what you cannot see
behind the rags, beyond the skin
color…brown
brown as the earth I'm standing on

What I have, I have earned
with dignity
I have earned your respect
because I am
Mex – I – Can!

All Our Brown-Skinned Angels

No human being
has the right to deprive
others from their freedom

but we live amongst people
who carry stones
instead of hearts

hatred on their tongues
These descendants of colonizers'
racist agenda

is always to get rid of those
that don't fit their way of being
Fear and threats are their weapons

laws such as HB 56 and SB 1070
imposed by judges and rulers
to carry out ethnic cleansing

to eradicate from our soil
all our brown-skinned angels
all our brown-skinned angels

Our skin is not dirty
Our language is not obscene
We are not garbage

The sun shines the same
on all people
no matter how they treat us

We will no longer run
from our oppressors

We will not hide

If we must fight
we will defend ourselves
by our united hearts

Our strength is in our blood
in our voice, in our history
We are warriors, *Mexica tiahui*!

Cliff's Edge

You and I hold hands by cliff's edge
watch the ships sail
with the crossing breeze
admire the ancient archipelago

If tomorrow we lose our sight
become completely blind
we could stand still by the edge
of this cliff
for the wind will show us how

Hear me now—
you and I are born from such mysteries

Dandelion

My daughter and I wrote a poem last night
We picked ideas and objects to write about
We mixed them up
in a salad bowl
carefully tossed

We picked funny words
to make happy sounds
We added, repeated, deleted

We laughed and fell to our knees
pretended to be dandelions
waiting for the wind
to shake us up

We acted like daffodils
and tulips soaked in rain
We opened ourselves in the morning
and closed our petals
when the sun ran away

We agreed that our poem
should be like a dandelion
so when shared with others
the words will float to the ears
of those who listen

Carried by our breath
like the dandelion fuzzes
in the breeze
and so, my daughter and I
wrote a poem last night

Flower Girl

My daughter decorates the driveway
with a carpet of flowers. She cuts *Pieris japonica*
purple and white grape hyacinth
viburnum leaves and *Ligustrum* buds until
summertime roses come into bloom

In India, creating a carpet of flowers
is a custom to welcome visitors

To me it is a sign of something else—
that my daughter had lived previous lifetimes
How else can I explain?

Her kindness, her love for others, her
warm welcome to our blue house

My daughter has no wings
but she is an angel with brown skin

Ten Years Gone

in memory of my son,
Késhava Kumara Sánchez 9-3-1987 to 7-9-2000

I could not
teach my son
how to be a man

he'll always
be
a boy

standing by the water's edge
smiling
in that photograph

I speak his name
I speak his name
in silence

My Father Was a Bracero

I know this:
my father was a bracero
I hold his contract

yellow paper full
of restrictions
and prohibitions

his pay stub
not enough to survive
I wonder what he had to endure

I wonder if the DDT sprayed
on his face over the years
contributed to his ailments—

diabetes, asthma, the cerebral embolism
that blinded him
Laying railroad tracks

expanding commerce routes
from Texas, Alabama
Mississippi, Louisiana

My father's dried sweat merged
with that soil
under a burning sun

another nail on the ties
He went back to *Mexico-Tenochtitlán*
started a restaurant

so he could send me
to a private American school
He wanted me to learn

their language
to live way north
across the border line

He didn't want me to live
by my strong back, my strong arms
but by my words

II
Poems from
When There Were No Borders

*What's the world for you if you can't
make it up the way you want it?*
—Toni Morrison, *Jazz*

Itlapaltin nemiliztli

xiknechmachati, nemiliztli!
chichiltik uikpa tlakatilistli iuan estli
in texotli-xoxoktiiuik iluikatlampa
iuan in ueyameh
kostik tlasohtla in tonatiu iuan ikoxisentli
kamiltitlalli, atoctli
lalaxtletl, tlaixpoloani, maciticayotl
teixtlaltemiani, poktli mochiua
in youalli iuan in mictlan
santepan,
istaiuiomimeh iuan tlakuepalistli

Colores de la vida

(*Inspirado por el significado Maya de los colores*)

Muéstrame la vida!
Rojo de sangre y nacimiento
Azul-verde de los cielos
Y los océanos
Amarillo como el sol y el maíz tierno
Café de la tierra y los campos fértiles
Anaranjado como el fuego destructor
Purificante
El cegador humo gris
Se convierte
En la obscuridad de la noche
Y el inframundo
Finalmente,
El blanco de los huesos y el cambio.

Colors of Life

(Inspired by the Mayan significance of color)

Show me, life!
Red for birth and blood
Blue-green of the heavens
And the oceans
Yellow like the sun and ripe corn
Brown earth, fertile pastures
Orange fire, destroyer, purifier
Blinding gray smoke becomes
The blackness of the night and the underworld
Finally,
White of bones and change.

Mexica Tiahui

I walked the steps where priests,
Zapotec kings, left footprints, rituals
performed to invisible gods
Mictlantecuhtli, Mictecacíhuatl
rulers of the underworld and all living things.
Their energy emanating through temple stones carved,
shaped vestiges of reverence to nature and culture found
two centuries before the Spanish arrived, these standing
monuments proof of our undefeated spirit and struggle
Zapotec, Toltec, Olmec, Mayan, Aztec cultures
proof to the world that our ancestors were
intelligent people,
knowledgeable, cultured,
devout beings in harmony
with the universe,
life and death.
The sun shines its light upon us
as we follow the moon path
to rivers where we will survive.
We will never perish.
MEXICA TIAHUI

Cintéotl

Goddess of corn grown
from earth, rain and sun
kernels boiled nixtamal
grinding corn into dough
amasando
smoothing the dough

her soft hands soften the masa
grabbing a handful
left hand to right hand
begin to clap, clap, clap
from one damp hand to the other
her fingers stiff

with the slightest cup
and spring to the palm
clap and turn, clap and turn
lay it on the comal
flipped over
to cook the other side—

my mother's hands,
her spirit evoked
when I cook
aroma of fresh tortillas
fragrant and moist
remembering the sound

of her hands,
clap and turn,
clap and turn.

My Tongue / Mi lengua

My tongue retains the roaring sound of rivers, of the earth
    after the rain
falling over leaves, branches and flowers.

My tongue is stained with the juice of sweet pitayas, red,
    delicious, grown
under Tonatiuh's rays, our father sun.

My tongue reveres nature and all living beings, mountains,
    rivers, oceans, night and day.
My tongue wears Quetzal feathers, mystical birds from the
    Mayan paradise.

My tongue is impregnated with Calpulli, Tonalli, Xochitl,
    Xochipilli,
Mictlantecuhtli, Cuauthémoc, Moctezuma, Quetzalcoatl,
    Tomatl, Cintéotl.

My tongue speaks of temples, demigods, copal, flowers,
    medicinal plants,
jade masks, golden pectorals, obsidian stones, volcanoes,
    and blood.

My ancient tongue speaks Zapotec, Nahuatl, Purépecha,
    Tzotzil, Otomi,
Chamula, Mayan, Tarahumara.

My tongue is my identity—the connection to my people,
    my roots, my culture.
My language is from the earth, from the heavens, from
    my soul.

My tongue speaks, my soul feels the breath of the earth,
the sound of the wind Ehecatl.

Smoke

A tribute to Grandma Carmen

When I was a young child, my grandmother cleansed my body,
with herbs and smoke.

She swiftly brushed my body with ramas de pirul and flowers
red ribbon held,

the willow branches she brushed, brushed,
brushed away.

My stretched limbs—bad energy away
from me.

Fragrant sap remained on fingers dark
from cutting,

herbs frankincense chunks
burning copal—

Top, down, left, right her eyes closed.
Cleansing smoke.

Branches swirled the smoke,
with every stroke—

shaking filtering negative energy
the room full of smoke—

cleansing smoke
chasing evil spells—

silent prayer whisper
echoed, through the smoke,

she opened her eyes
two moons behind the clouds.

She wrapped the loaded branches
told me to throw them, behind my back—

and walk away—
into the light.

Milagros

Have you ever pinned down
a milagro on the cloth

of your favorite saint?
Tiny silver and brass charms offered

to thank for blessings received.
A house for the broken home,

A split heart for lost love,
praying for the lover to come back.

A hand for the injured laborer,
or the writer that can't write.

A mouth for those who speak
ill words praying they'll heal.

A foot to complete the journey,
to be able to move around,

unconfined unassisted.
A body for the departed,

or for the living wishing
they'd come home safe,

after deployment
to wars on foreign lands.

And the migrants
crossing deserts,

to arrive safe
to the promised land.

Or their home
away from this world.

Milagros, testimony of love
a promise of faith and hope.

1960

Five years young or younger
I was standing, walking…
Black-and-white photos taken
now fading in the memory of my past—

Growing up at my mom and dad's
restaurant right next to the biggest
bullfighting arena in the world,
Plaza México! where everything began.

Meanwhile, Jack Kerouac
getting high in my city.
Jazz poet, 242 blues choruses written
in an afternoon jam session.

"*& I came back Spitting Pulque in Borracho Ork
Saloons of old Sour Aztec Askin for more…*"

My father enrolled me in a private American School
Escuela Rikards from kindergarten to 5th grade.
My best friends then were Sally, Dick and Spot.
Scared of Santa Claus, learned about Halloween,

before I revered the Day of the Dead.
Once, I stole two hours from a day
I don't remember the week,
month or year, but I did it.

It was the day when I put the early bird songs
in my pocket after listening—
to the sound of young ladies,
clicking heels and castanets,

with amorous echoes nailed down—
to the soulless songs sung
by drunken patrons
at the restaurant my father owned—

where the jaguars don't stop
nor the wounded beggars
nor the condors descending
from the Andes' higher peaks.

I stole two hours—
I filled them with roses, words,
feelings and metaphor,
rhyme, and me—

above the subway
below the heavens
of this earth
where I stood still.

Show Me Your Papers

I will show you my papers.
Which ones first?
Old yellow papers dated 1944

My father's papers Atchinson Railway man
bracero hard work *con* pride
he worked here during the war

my *abuelo*'s yellow pay stubs
from the Yuma farm scorching heat
Tío Manuel's pay stub too small

Imperial Valley lettuce land
what papers you want to see
first and last.

My ID driver license
legal document to move around?
My wedding certificate?

Testimony to my wife—
and all my vows.
My kids' birth certificates

born in this land.
Social Security card?
My paycheck stub?

Taxes, taxes, taxes!
Take-home pay too low
who wants to know?

You want to see my papers?
My notebook? My poems
telling my story—

Papers with new laws
deny my existence
because some papers

don't tell it all
my dignity my pride is
not printed on *THOSE* papers

those papers will burn!
Why do you want to see my papers?

Cuando no había fronteras / When There Were No Borders

From a conversation with the former US Poet Laureate Juan Felipe Herrera, Richard Hugo House, November 22, 2019

We talked about quelites, watercress and herbs
good for the body and mind and the memories
embedded in the fibers of acociles, esquites, elotes
and all that we left behind.
Not a coincidence but a cultural fact
when we learned that nuestros abuelos, padres,
tíos y primos crossed "la línea" to harvest the land
from the Yuma fields, Tulare's groves, Louisiana cotton
cattle and horses, Colorado, Idaho, Nevada farms.
They worked the season and then went back
before snow and frost covered the ground.
Too cold en el Norte, heading South to sun-land.
We agreed that en aquel entonces, back then
"Cuando no había fronteras", when there were no borders
they crossed, worked, and went back. That's it!
Back then "we were not shadows, now we walk through
    the shadows."
History has been forgotten. What was dignified then
is now a criminal act, a death sentence equals the desire
to live, to be free, to be happy, to speak their mind.
We belong to this ancestral land.

Life / Vida

these days filled with lies	*mentiras,*
fear, intimidation smoke screens,	*humo*
nebulous particles we breath	*respiramos*
inhale deep, because we need	*aire*
air to live—	*vida*
the orange glow	*resplandor*
father sun, Tonatiuh	*sol*
remains in the center—	*el centro—*
while the planet floats	*flota*
we make the earth turn,	*vueltas*
the rhythm of our heartbeat	*latido*
our pulsing heart	*corazón*
the size of a postcard stamp	*estampilla*
stuck on the map	*pegada*
of our existence	*existencia*
the cycle repeats itself	*se repite*
the cycle begins once more	*continua*
when night falls, we rest	*descansamos*
our soul,	*alma*
to see the light	*luz*
the new wind of change,	*viento nuevo*
the new day.	*el nuevo día*

Nationalization

assimilation	feminization	constitution
concentration	masturbation	coalition
saturation	ejaculation	collision
polarization	prostitution	evolution
gentrification	satisfaction	communication
population	connection	satiation
proliferation	reflection	modernization
discrimination	validation	simplification
repatriation	education	naturalization
repudiation	socialization	negation
immigration	indoctrination	vindication
consolidation	separation	retribution
deportation	manifestation	sedation
fascination	revolution	eradication
legalization	proclamation	irrigation
conciliation	emancipation	beautification
invasion	colonization	simulation
pollution	predomination	distribution
fumigation	evangelization	filtration
reflection	humanization	aggravation
confusion	contamination	in our nation

Wind

Invisible men

Stand outside

Home Depot

Only the wind

Knows

Their names

Sanctuary

for José Robles

His crime is—
his desire is to live with dignity.
He is undocumented,
doesn't need a license to live,
is the anchor of his family.

A painter by trade, he wears an ankle monitor,
sits on the concrete bench,
behind the iron gate,
he doesn't want to be deported.
He smokes a cigarette.

Looks up to the sky seeking solace.
He watches the painters across 9th.
Misses his family, his friends, watches TV.
He feels like a caged lion,
paces back and forth.

He stops—listens, to people talking out in the street,
feels he is in purgatory.
Now, in sanctuary, in a lilac basement,
sheltered in a sacred place a man lives,

while he waits and waits.
Knows he cannot change his past,
he cannot defy ICE.
Doesn't want to risk his family,
gets horrible headaches.

Was assaulted, kicked in the head.
His body slammed on concrete,
lives in fear—
in fear for his daughters, alone with their mother.

The caged lion roars in silence.

He paces and paces and paces behind secure walls,
a prisoner whose only crime is to be human.

Your Body

I want to surf your body
ride every curl, curve and crevice
I want to trace every tattoo
beginning with the rose's stem
on your ankle.

I want to entwine
the vine
running up
your thighs
with the tip of my tongue.

I want to lick the nectar
of your blossoming
love
one drop at a time
I will release the butterflies

in your womb.
I want to get lost in your hills
your valleys, your highways.
I need no compass
I will follow

the sparkle in your eyes
the stars in your hair
cascading down
your shoulders
your hips.

I'm seasoned wood.
I want to burn
in your fire
of desire
let the blinding smoke

shroud our embrace.

Three Words

Today was a stormless day,
faint drizzle at best.
Tempered sunlight,
front railing stained.

No UPS packages,
no bags left outside,
no messages on the phone,
no problems tonight.

Fresh veggies for supper
cooked down slow,
flavor of the land
and the hands that sowed the seed.

Those hands, tender hands
always give, even what they don't have.
Those soft hands belong,
to an angel in disguise

with golden hair and green eyes
to whom I say
every chance I get,
I love you—

all the time.

Poets' Temple

I would like to see a Temple for Poets
where every Sunday the sermon
begins with Walt Whitman's "Leaves of Grass,"
followed by Yeats's "A Dialogue of Self and Soul"
and William Blake's "The Angel."

Ezra Pound will make the sharp distinction
between literary and esoteric traditions.
May Sarton will jump in to tell us how it is.

William Carlos Williams will debate her points.
Neruda will bring understanding
to the words we heard.
Meanwhile, Federico García Lorca
will stand in the pulpit, to tell us about "La aurora."

Cuando *"llega y nadie la recibe en su boca*
porque allí no hay mañana ni esperanza posible…
La luz es sepultada por cadenas y ruidos."

Solemn music echoes in the atrium
when the modern poets, the beats walk in
like the saints did at one time.
In the line we see—
Ginsberg, Kerouac, Marty Matz, Bukowski.

Books in hand
ready to let the words f l y in the air,
the music in their voices fills the space

and all of us bow down
to our muses
glorifying the words, sound,
metaphor and rhyme,
where poetry lives and shines!

Excuse Me Absent Poet But…

I wonder,
if you ever wrote anything
about the silhouette trees make
or the sounds unheard when instruments
are played? The cries of hungry people.
The snoring of alcoholics sleeping in doorways.
Torn knee ligaments, steam boiler ignitions.
Silent conversations in crowded malls.
Tapping shoes rhythmically
at the beat of jazz or blues.
Leaves on branches
high. Crows' ear-
s p l i t t i n g
h u bb u b.
C a t s
purring,
dogs
dreaming,
fish
breathing,
in the
water,
tanked,

silent.

Have you ever heard those sounds, dear absent poet?
I've heard them all
tonight.

Selecting a Reader

*Cento poem composed with titles from
James Bertolino's* New & Selected Poems
Carnegie Mellon University Press, 1978
(*For Jim on his birthday*)

The Teacher selected the Snow Angel
Beyond the Storm as if Bound
in Liquid Moonlight.
The Night was Smooth but The Cold Room.
Day of Change when the Yellow Spring,
Spring Thaw: Fish, The Scavenge
Woke The Flower and the Barefoot Lover
The Landscape filled with Lizards and Gulls
Salmon Fishing, Boundary Bay,
That December Thirteen. Storms, Relentless
To The Hum, Seventeen Year Locust created
The Story of The Sacrifice that made the day.
Something Familiar, a Song for the Unborn
Extending Foreground, The Marriage
at Memorial Park at Sunrise.
The Veteran, The Baker were present,
even the girl wearing The Red Dress who said:
I wish I Had a Packard, The Pleasure of The Italians.
After the Climb and Love's Body Consumed,
Notes for an Elegy mentioned the Talisman.
In the Portrait: My American Man, all the Changes
expressed, The Blood Vision through the Blue Bottle.
Employed, I sold a Poem titled: The Pothole Sonnet
based On a Line by John Ashbery.

A New Star in the Darkened Sky

For my first son, Vaisnava Gosai Sánchez
(June 11, 1984–February 11, 2020)
We are a deck of cards someone else shuffled,
we are thrown into the world,
the gamble of life.

We learn to walk, to live. Each step is a story and
each story is a new star in the heaven of our memory.
    —Rubén Blades

I remember the day he was born
the years when the three of us
jumped and laughed at silly jokes,
the years when he would smell dandelions
because for a child everything is beautiful.

I remember, he loved to wear
my Mickey Mouse T-shirt.
Back in '88 he won the "cutest kid" photo contest.

I remember—
He begot a daughter at 17.
He tried to be a man on his own.
However the divorce separated us all.
He had a rough time in this world,
he lost one of his younger brothers
Keshava Kumara under the Wyoming sun.

I remember—
the blown tire, tragic disaster
I remember :: I remember it all.
He was unharmed, but not his brother
now gone.

He was only eleven years young,
too young.

I remember—
the laughter, their made-up words
like "Sarkolaks" the ruler of the fable he wrote.
Horses, shields and swords
the aspiring king that wanted to save the world.

Death comes unannounced,
silently, in the light of day or in the darkest nights.

A child that never saw
the wonders of this world.
Now both join hands,
to once again, walk the thorny path.

Gosai's beautiful life didn't shine as I wish it had,
a victim of his own vice.

The memories come back
like the sound of rumble strips
driving at night.

Sometimes they sound
like living water dripping into the void.

Not all of us were born under the same stars.
Some are brighter than others,
such mystery I can't define.

Reminiscing

Me and my Impala
cruising Hollywood,
tilting at Crenshaw
rear tail tilt at Western

left side up at Vine
past Cahuenga
all the way to Las Palmas
straight up at Highland

cops lurking for dragging
sparkling tail pipes
grinding,
bandanas hanging

Pendleton high-button shirts
flowing.
José, Chuco, Rudy and me
riding *ranflas*

on lower-than-low
Hollywood streets.
We cruise the night
riding high in purple 1965

Chevy Impala
custom paint,
crushed velvet seats,
smooth ride—

the pride of the hood.
Tierra, El Chicano,
Third World music blasting
speakers loud

we scratch our way back
to Atlantic Boulevard
East Los *El Chante,* homes!
Homies got to sleep too, *ése*!
Hangover morning deal
menudo, pozole, *birongas.*
Tonight we cruise downtown
Main and Broadway our way

across the river.
Low riding, riding low
riding *ranflas*
on lower-than-low American streets.

Borinquen

Clave's rhythm takes me inward,
in unison con *la sangre*, Taíno blood.
I feel the hot sun kissing my skin,
while Atlantic Ocean waves kiss *Borinquen's* feet.
"*La Isla del Encanto.*"

La Pachanga begins up on Cañaboncito Hills.
El ritmo de plena me sigue con cuatro, pandero y güiro.
Pa' Ponce, Mayagüez, Bayamón y Caguas voy.
Vega Alta y Vega Baja también voy.

Palm trees sway with salsa rhythm,
Tito Puente's timbales beat,
echo from San Juan to *Nueva York*.
Tonight I'm gonna play *guaguancó* y rumba
like Ray Barretto, "*Manos Duras*" did back in the heydays
of boogaloo *con ritmo y sabor*!

I will read Victor Hernández Cruz while
sipping *café en pocillo*.
I walked Old San Juan's cobblestone streets
to find boricuas playing dominos.
In my mind, I imagine Martín Espada *pregonando*—

en La Calle San Sebastián:
Alabanza! para ellos
Alabanza! para Puerto Rico
Alabanza! para Borinquen

A ritmo de bomba me voy, pa' Carolina
where Roberto Clemente was born.
Desde el Yunque mi coquí canta happy midnight songs,
to serenade my tropical dreams.

Héctor Lavoe, "*El Cantante de los Cantantes*" walked down
Calle Luna, Calle Sol. His distant voice reverberates.
Look who's coming down Calle Cristo!
It is Willie Colón playing his trombone!

Mi china waits for me
at the *colmado con la fruta guindando*
near *Parada veintidós* where we had lunch *para dos.*
*Asopao, tostones, pasteles y mofongo de concha
con un palito de ron!*
Barrilito pol favol, Señol. Ay Bendito!

Up in El Morro's tallest tower my flag waves,
blessing *mi tierra santa, tierra pura*
que con toda su hermosura
has given me infinite pleasure—

En Bellas Artes "El Jíbaro" Andrés Jiménez
cantando a los boricuas ausentes:
"*Viva mi bandera, viva mi nación*
Vivan los boricuas que son boricuas de corazón."

Found Sonnets

Walking my dog one cold rainy night,
my two feet behind four paws ahead of mine,
we walked the parking lot without fright
or hesitation, knowing we were fine;
suddenly the dog stopped to find
muddied polyester fiber-filled headless
plush toys someone left behind:
dog, bear, rabbit, dolls abandoned, neat no less—
clothes strewn, toothbrush, hairbrush all on the ground,
schoolbooks, notebooks, paperbacks' wet
discarded stories, fiction unfound.
I picked up a book, left others with much regret:
garbage to some, but *Shakespeare's Sonnets*?
Still dry for me to enjoy all the canzonets!

My Experience at the Detention Center and Why I Became Interested in Mentoring the Youth in Detention

There are seeds that are blown by the wind.
There are seeds that are planted by human beings.
Those seeds will grow into beautiful flowers and trees.
Those are the powerful seeds of knowledge mankind needs.

The seeds will germinate, throwing
roots expanded like fingers, grabbing hold of the earth.
The roots contain well-being, grandiosity,
wisdom, virtue, truth, pride, glory,

faith, harmony, agreement, disagreement,
tranquility, ancestry, principle.
The roots will give way to the branches,
providing leaves, foliage, and fruit.

Reason, must be at the base of all that flourishes.
Think of the dervishes' dance,
who whirl and whirl away.
There is a cosmic dance throughout the human forest,

where we encounter people from different places
with different faces.
I am one of those trees. I unraveled my branches—
to provide fruit and shelter to the seeds I planted.

These days I share fruit and shelter with the
youth in perilous situations. Compassion
and an open heart are the tools I use to help them
free themselves from the trauma and pain in their heart.

Poetry is the ax I use to remove
the stumps that hold them down.

The words come out of their hearts like seeds,
germinating to create their own poems, poetry,

they didn't realize they already had.
When the young are praised,
their faces gleam like the sunshine in the early spring.
Their poems are gems, strung together like diamonds,
after the rain.

National Poem in Your Pocket Day

April 30th, 2020

We are the human forest
where all the trees
are different.
Yet we all share
the same sun
the same air
the same rain
the same soil
where all
our roots connect with each other.
We are the human forest.

Kubota Garden, Seattle

There is a conversation in the silent garden.
    Laceleaf Japanese maple whispers stories
in summer moonlight to the azaleas and rhododendrons.
    Camellia blossoms by the stone vase glow,
    dazzle waves of pale green and red.
Burning bush leaves remind us winter is coming.
    Two stone bridges united across the pond
resemble unity—over their reflection,
    like humans crossing bridges walk the hidden paths,
sending forget-me-nots to their familial pink fallen petals.
    In the garden, the sun yearns to cross the moon bridge,
and merge with the heart bridge, covered in snow.
    Here all the flowers speak a different language.
Each petal, a different story.
    Yet, all share the same soil, same sun, same air.
Plants and trees living in harmony, like humans should be.

Ode to an Oak Tree

*"When the oak is felled the whole forest echoes
   with its fall,
but a hundred acorns are sown in silence by an
   unnoticed breeze."*
         —Thomas Carlyle

Acres of aging grand trees on the lower ground,
boughs bending, rising and falling with the wind,
randomly sinking and fainting responsive bird songs,
dry ground covered with heart-shaped leaves and twigs.
At night, the trees on the higher ground cast
their shadow under the clear moonlight.
Your branches blown by the east-west wind,
secrets told when the birds can't sleep.
Full moon filled with countenance, dense,
murky clouds, wreaths of fragrant pines.
Oak and cedar limbs swish with the wind brushed,
your very old mystical greatness stands.
Looking at the stars and the gorgeous clouds
in summertime, your sun-drenched splendor
shelters birds hanging on your moist branches,
crows, blue jays, chickadees and eagle nests.
Nakedly standing in spring your dormant roots
thaw below the frozen ground.
Do not say that the roots are weak,
these roots are strong, the very roots of being.

Oda a un roble viejo

*"Cuando el roble es talado todo el bosque le hace eco
    a su caída,
pero cien bellotas son sembradas en silencio por una
    brisa inadvertida."*
                        —*Thomas Carlyle*

El valle está lleno de acres de grandiosos árboles ancestrales
el viento sacude las ramas, arriba y abajo casi doblándose.
Las aves responden con canciones al azar que se hunden y
    desmayan
en tierra seca cubierta de ramas y hojas en forma de corazón.
De noche, los árboles en cerro proyectan
su sombra bajo la clara luz de la luna.
Tus ramas agitadas por el viento de este a oeste,
secretos que se cuentan cuando los pájaros no pueden
    dormir.
Luna llena con rostro de tristeza, densas
nubes turbias, fragrantes guirnaldas de pino.
Las ramas del roble y cedro crujen con el viento
cepillando tu infalible antigua grandeza mística.
Mirando las estrellas y las hermosas nubes,
en verano, tu esplendor empapado por el sol
da refugio a las aves que cuelgan en tus ramas húmedas,
cuervos, carboneros, arrendajos azules y nidos de águila.
En la primavera tus raíces latentes desnudamente
se deshielan, por debajo del suelo congelado.
No digan que las raíces son débiles,
estas raíces son fuertes, las mismas raíces del ser.

Greensward

> *Treat the earth well. It was not given to you by*
> *your parents...*
> *it is loaned to you by your children.*
> *—Kenyan Proverb*

Where the pavement meets the gravel road,
> leaves of grass and dandelion moons grow.

The open meadow opens to western hemlock,
> Pacific madrone,

black cottonwood trees release translucent fuzzes
> twirling, falling down on nursing log sustaining life.

New saplings grow within the wounded tree,
> trunk leaning toward the sound

of the shallow stream where blackberry bushes,
> ivy, tall grass live.

Up above the canopy spotted towhee sings
> while crows and swallows fly from branch to branch.

A symphony gleaming lulled by the breeze, weaving,
> soft emotion, warmth of the early spring.

And the birds sing, melodious noise along
> the luminous path across the open meadow.

Slow walk around the edge, step by step
> meditating on the tinkling dewy grass,

the glowing verdant leaves, a green oasis
> away from the rumbling sound of city streets.

Césped

Trata bien la tierra. Tus padres no te la dieron...
tus hijos te la prestaron.
      —*Kenyan Proverb*

Donde el pavimento se encuentra con la grava
    el césped y las lunas de diente de león crecen.

El prado abierto le da paso al cicuta occidental,
    y también al árbol madrone del Pacífico.

Los árboles de algodón negro liberan su pelusa translúcida
    girando, cayendo sobre el tronco decadente que
        mantiene la vida.

Nuevos árboles crecen dentro del árbol herido,
    tronco inclinado en dirección hacia el murmullo

del riachuelo donde los arbustos de moras,
    hiedra, y yerbas altas crecen.

Por encima del dosel el towhee manchado canta,
    mientras que los cuervos y las golondrinas vuelan de
        rama en rama.

Una brillante sinfonía adormecida por la brisa tejiendo,
    tiernamente la emoción de la temprana primavera.

Y los pájaros cantan, ruido melodioso a lo largo
    del camino luminoso que atraviesa el campo verde.

Caminando lentamente a lo largo del borde, paso a paso
    meditando en el rocío de la hierba tintineante,

las brillantes hojas verdes semejan un oasis verdoso
   lejos del ruido estruendoso de las calles de la ciudad.

before I'm gone

before I'm gone I want to visit
all the places that hold
memories of my youth

before I'm gone
I want to hug my friends
and squeeze their hands

before I'm gone
I want to see my sons
and my daughter once more

before I'm gone
I want to hear my poet friends
read their best work

before I'm gone
I want to touch the temple stones
aztec mayan olmec

before I'm gone
I want to visit my father
and my mother's grave

before I'm gone
I want to write
one last poem

before I'm gone
I want to have the last dance
with my loving wife

before I'm gone

III
NEW POEMS:
When We Were Water

*Poetry does not consist in saying everything,
but in making one dream everything.*
—Charles Augustin Sainte-Beuve,
Causeries du Lundi

Art Is Life

Everything found in nature is art.
Colorful shapes, mysterious as the windswept landscapes.
Old-growth trees whose branches sweep the wind
repeating the stories sung by hawks, eagles,
gulls, blue jays, chickadees, hummingbirds and crows.

Their feathers flutter as they fall, softly,
like dandelion fuzzies landing gently on the hard ground.
The spark within the human mind ignites,
with color and light describing the beauty,
the calm, the ebb and flow of the ocean waves.

Art can reveal those mysteries.
Like the ovary, pistil, filament, and anther of a flower.
Only the artist can describe through music and song.
The poet uses his senses to paint the sky with words.
The artist's brush paints what he/she feels.

The dancer dances interpreting such art.
Art is the language of the soul.

Bean Around the Globe

At the Black Dragon Café, Victoria, BC

Thelonious Monk looks over iPod playlist,
Aztec and Cuban organic beans,
burlap sacks stamped Guatemalan direct trade
from Santa Clara Estate,
Guatemalan coffee hills.

Slowly roasting while…

Leonard Cohen sings
Hallelujah, Hallelujah, Hallelujah,
Halleluu-uuu-uu-jah
speakers high—democracy on the ground—

Ground beans release roasted aroma,
Arabica bean fragrance black hot soothing taste!

Casa Ruíz—Boquete, Pánama
Hacienda La Esperanza.

Jimmy Buffett *Havana Daydreamin'*
bolsters songs midafternoon coffee
lunch grilled cheese and spinach pie

Grace Kelly on table scratched looks sideways, she whispers:
*"hey now, he's just another lover,
he's just another lover goodbye"*

Coffee dripping out on one side of my mouth
as the black-coat lady with spiderweb stockings
walked by…

her black heels clack, clack, clack as she walked
wooden floors, the New Era of King Curtis
rose above beyond sex wax and Kilauea surfboard dreams.
Floating dragons, spinning cycles high on Ethiopia Harrar
climbed up Tikal's highest temple to see beyond Inca gold—

Latte Americano embedded on brick walls.
Listening to the Fabulous Ginn Sisters songs
lingering on ceiling high
coffee aromas float
perfect afternoon to sip and write,
coffeehouse in the middle
narrow alley Canadian Chinatown.

Whisper

Does it matter if I don't write a poem today?
Who's keeping track?
No one I suppose.
But if I write something just because
it's part of my daily practice,
will it matter if I don't stick to any rules?

Oh, wait a minute…
What about the birds?
The dream I forgot when the thunderbirds
opened their wings,
uprooted trees, crumbling to dust.
Charmed ocean waves paused.

No breeze tonight,
soon the pink moon will rise.
Neither the weeping willow nor the
absent nightingale will get in the way
of the thunderbird waves of fire.
Raising up to the sky!

The sleeping infant separated
from the mother's breast.
Will the twinkling stars wake him up again?
It's hard to tell when the moon
began to sing in
her soprano voice.

Healing sound for the spent daffodils,
the drooping tulips and the dying lilies.
I lose consciousness and sleep again,
charmed by the sounds of the lute
the organ and the clavichord.
A new poem is a new miracle.

Guatemalan Miracle

For me, birthdays are not a big deal,
only the milestones count.
One step at a time, is the safest way
to get around.
I walked many roads, many paths—
spiritual and physical alike.
I continue to walk among people
who appreciate my work,
the work I've done so far.
And the human that I am.
So, what's another birthday…

I may ask, but a chance to continue
sharing my vision of the world with the young.
I never imagined having fathered three sons
and now to have none.
Destiny had its own plan, which wasn't mine.
The scars on my skin, the punctures in my soul,
the aches on my bones.
There have been situations, confrontations,
explanations, appropriations
that have led to conversations—
the remorse and regret for things undone.

Still kept in my heart.

One day we heard the call,
we opened the door when adoption knocked.
Loud and friendly.
We were blessed
with a new seedling

which has grown to be a woman
still growing into her own future,
educated, hopeful.

A Guatemalan miracle that warmed our hearts and souls.

Daffodils and Dandelions

In a sea of green, tall green grass,
yellow buoys stand.
Some high, some low.
Not all the daffodils grow in groups,
unlike the dandelions.
Perhaps their roots are different.

The dandelions unlike the daffodils
have medicinal benefits.
The daffodils are gorgeous,
always ready to kiss the sun.
But the dandelion provides more than kisses.
It can heal from within,

yellow medicine from the ground up.

Washing the Dishes

Breakfast done.
Scrubbing dirt and grime from glasses smudged.
My mind wanders off, away from the current,
the flow, the worries, the plans, the doubts.

Soaped sponge, scrubbing brush,
water pouring clear,
slippery plates and cups,
midnight teacup empty.

Water, cleansing water, purifying element,
one part oxygen, two parts hydrogen.
Some waters become holy,
depending on their origin.

For me, washing dishes is an act of renewal,
repentance, reverence, and surrender.
Our world needs it as much as our
bodies and souls.

I scrub and rinse the daily grime away.

Monk's Dream on Monet's *Nymphéas bleus*

In a dream splashed
with purple notes
tenor sax lilies float
a masterpiece in blue.

Monk strikes high octave
light changes soft tone
snare drums turn lilies
color, soft shadows

behind the double bass
purple pond dream in blue
Monk's *bleus*,
Monet's world.

Only a Dream

Last night you entered my dream
with the sound of violins and cellos
very slowly like Aaron Copland's
Appalachian Spring

Then you, yes you changed the tone
cracked the dream open
the way Beethoven played piano
in "Emperor" Rondo: Allegro

I floated with you above the ceiling high
cracked the ceiling through
dissipated in the cold air of night
to find myself wet, after the rain

woken up by the pink tongue
of the dog on my lips
reminding me I have to go to work
under the rain and the sweet floating dream of you.

We Danced

we danced
in the cloud

of music
our arms

around
each other

our feet
moved swiftly

to the left
to the right

stirring the dust
fallen

from the stars
on the tiled floor

sparkled bright
by the light outside

Visit to Dachau

July 6th, 2014

We crossed the threshold of death
at the iron gate marked
"Arbeit Macht Frei"
Work will set you free

dense air, weather-stained rocks
where the barracks were
release earth's heat
mirage of what used to be

barbed wire still there
electric fence still there
the ditch still there
barking dogs, guards with whips gone

what remains in the air
is still there.
Forced labor, bodies—nothing but
skin and bones

skin and bones
worked under the sun
died in the cold
outdoor poles bodies hung

naked, punished
hands tied
their souls lost
dead man lying unknown.

Busy black ants moving to and fro
burrowing in and out of their holes
laborious insects like the humans
that lived there before

could they be those humans?
Reincarnated trapped in the same land
where they lived and died
waiting to be free?

Today I Killed a Spider—Accidentally

Today I killed a spider
una araña patraña
que salió del caño

my daughter's violin practice
halted—screeched on the A note
como uñas en el pizarrón

y gritó! Ay papi! Una araña
en la pared, the wall I said
sí, can't you see?

Ponte tus lentes
put on your glasses
see the eight giant legs

allí mírala creeping
crawling waiting to jump
en mi cara! Get it out of here

sácala, matala, cuelgala de una riata
please take it outside
déja que coma moscas y mosquitos

but please take it out of the house.
I grabbed a damp towel
se la eché encima

y la araña patraña was caught
asfíxiated en la toalla
pobrecita sin dos patas

my karma is not good now
because today I killed a spider
accidentally, lo siento mucho.

I'm so sorry.

By the line of the spine

*Poem composed of titles from books found on level 7
of the spiral in the Seattle Public Library*

Who's who of the conquistadors?
Where the desert meets the sea,
Beyond the land of the North Umpquas
And the valley of the rogues

The English in the Caribbean
The war of 1812
Recorded
in the diaries of two Ansbach Jaegers, who

Along with planters, paupers,
Cavaliers and pioneers,
Axe and bible at hand
Cried: "Give me liberty"

The Seminoles dwellers of the everglades,
Missions and pueblos of the southwest
Millennial kingdom of the Franciscans
And "The changing Indian"

No peace beyond the line.
Walkara, hawk of the mountains
Reveres the Indian leaders who helped shape America.
Ignored but not forgotten:

Life of Ma-ka-tai-me-she-kia-kiak
or Black Hawk's biography, dictated by himself.
Respect to the land
The only land I know.

Crack the Pot

Oh! How I wish
Mother Teresa was still around.
I can imagine her, holding a baseball bat
like those signed by Tony Armas.
She'd be swinging it against that piñata pot
thrashing candy, lollipops, while the kids
evade the bat and soon, *wham*!
Crack the pot, let the candy
fly!

Dear Papi

In Memory of Don Victor Sánchez Hernández, 1924–1967

I've been meaning to write you a letter.
But wasn't sure where to send it.
It's been 52 years since you've been away—
from this world.
It is a miracle that I'm alive
to tell your story and mine.
A spark departed your heart
when your body could no longer hold it.
It is a miracle for me to remember you
to know I'm not alone.

It is a miracle when you answer my call
after I talk to your photograph when I need guidance.
I miss you!
I have been missing you for a long time.
The lessons you taught me during my infancy
are well-kept and cherished.
They have been my support,
and have given me the strength necessary
to live and share my life with others.

There are many things I want to share with you.
Some of them I am very proud of,
others, not so much.
Life can bring many pleasant and unpleasant situations.
You know all about that.
I just want to touch base with you today, which is the day
when the world and my heart began to miss your touch,
your words, and your teachings.
I will be waiting for your visit on November 2nd
you know, that day is a very special day for miracles.

Dissolved

I held my breath
           when I heard   you were   dead
never   coming back
          to visit   to hang
                      around
at night   the blinking   lights
  show   strange   shadows
things   only   the   disappeared
       know   where they are

   your   ashes   are   now
  in   the   water,   the   river
ganga maiya,   dissolved,   merged

  d I s I n t e g r a t e d

  if   blood   could   speak
it would   yell   a   shriek
  it'd tell   your story,   our…story

  stored in   your   wrists,   ribs

  where   every   punch you received
is   marked   by a scar
  and   the tattoos   on your tender
  skin   punctured,   m a r k e d

     my breath,   your ashes
  rest   in   the   b o t t o m

of the reservoir, deep
      where   they   will   remain
until
t h e
r I v e rr
                   u
                        n
                              s   dry

Essential Heroes

And one day the world became a petri dish—
Someone's cough could be a death sentence.
Poisoned air, living air, dangerous air.
Scared; we listened, we followed,
we washed our hands, constantly—
We wore our smile behind the masks,
distanced, we lived in our cocoons.
Behind closed doors, windows shut.

Avoided everyone and anyone within six feet.
Panicked to get the mail, to put out the trash.
We listened, we cared, while others did not.
Some of us survived, yet we could not go outside.
Magically a hidden network was discovered!
Unnamed and independent workers became:
Essential, without a license!
A new brand of heroes, a new generation born.

The ordinary worker became a HERO!
An essential part of society.
The same society that sees them as ordinary
or undocumented and unskilled.
Yet, they became ESSENTIAL to all.
They worked not only because they needed money,
but because they could.
Risking their own lives for everyone else.

They delivered food, took care of elders and the disabled,
delivered packages, stocked shelves,
ran errands, changed sheets in hospitals.
Their low wages didn't keep them from working.
Essential workers, a name given to all who fought
against the virus.

They overcame their struggles and fears.
Some of them didn't survive.

The well-to-do experienced a cruel reality.
Pandemic purchases, even frivolous ones,
impossible without essential workers.
The essential worker became the banner word
that will endure as a moniker representing
unity, sacrifice, involvement,
interconnection, and care without prejudice
for all Americans.

February Snow

Radio broadcast: snow and frost
as we drove north on 35th.
I counted cold houses and empty
stores, blinking neon signs.

Overnight snow ground-covered
wilted weeds amid early crocuses
stubborn daffodils sprouting fingers
out of frozen ground.

This morning—
The ball of fire rose up behind the Cascades.
Coldness remains, birds hanging
on seed feeder,

still, front and backyard undone,
birdbath frozen,
snowman with punky hair
made out of leaves, rocks for eyes
pine branches for arms
and a chile pepper nose.
Our cold house
warmed by the fireplace burning

cedar and pine
warms up our spirit,
brightens up our lives
on a snowy February night.

For Don Victor Sánchez

Ye' huatl-in ta'tli / This Is My Father

When I hear certain sounds…
they echo the memory of my father,
when he was a young lad, mining
in Real del Monte silver mines.

Where silver dust settled in his lungs.

The sound of steel scratching, banging
brings back the memory
of the adult I knew,
steadfast, energetic, and always friendly.

Two relics of his I hold,
his bracero contract
and a yellow paper paystub,
taking "savings aside"

—they never got back.

Photos in sepia
vaguely show his features;
no need for clarity,
I can see him

clearly—
through my watery eyes.

I Miss the Rain

I love the sun shining on the windowpane
I love the sun by the seashore
I love the sun on the backyard
I love the heat on my skin

But on days like this I miss the rain.
Sometimes there is not enough rain

to color the garden green
the roses pink, apples red
sweeten the pears, plump the plums.
Sun and rain bring in summer's joy!

I Met a Brown-Skinned Angel

I always write and talk about being human with a heart instead of a stone. Today I had the chance to prove that. I walked out across the street from our house to begin my morning walk with the dog. I saw a man turning around the corner on 39th. He glanced at me, I looked back to notice he was wearing a familiar hat. A hat only seen in Patzcuaro Michoacán. He gently approached while donning his mask to ask if I spoke Spanish. I replied, yes of course. He asked me if I knew where the nearest Salvation Army Shelter was at. I told him there is one on Greenwood Ave., not far from here. Meanwhile, the dog is moaning telling me to go because he has "to go."

I felt something within me when he said, *I need to complete the fare for a bus ticket to Wenatchee*, a place in eastern WA where he could go to work and catch the last of the harvest time. He offered to rake the leaves in the front and backyard of our house after the windstorm we had last night. Told him we did not need that at the time. However, I said I'd like to help you as much as I can.

He spoke with a low-tone voice. I felt as if I was looking at my father in his eyes, for he was a migrant worker in his youth. He was a bracero who worked for the Sante Fe Railway Company. I want to call this man Manuel, I know he gave me his name, but I forgot. I felt compelled to help him out. I told him to wait for me at the park down the street where I could find him once I got back from my walk. I phoned my wife to share with her the experience so far.

At home, I fixed him a lunch bag, took sixty dollars out of our stash. Drove off to the park where he sat patiently waiting. Waved at him, invited him to get in the truck. Drove him downtown to King Street Station where he could get on a Greyhound. While I drove, we talked about the coronavirus pandemic, the political climate, and immigration. He replied with "dicen que," "people say" this and that. I thought he knew something about protection, infection, and cleanliness. I felt better sitting next to him knowing full well that I could be at risk. His humble approach and demeanor didn't scare me for I felt safe taking him where he needed to go. Definitively a man from the countryside who is trying to survive and work instead of begging, I truly like that, because migrants are not thieves, just humans in the landscape of our extensive tapestry of humanity across the land where no border, walls, chain-link fences will stop a human from being human among other humans. I value life, their willingness and determination regardless of their situation.

Money is nothing when it is used for a good cause. How much does it cost to save a man's life? Perhaps I am stretching the facts, but I honestly think, feel, that he IS/WAS an Angel in disguise. I did all that despite feeling achy since I was experiencing the effects of the first shingles shot in my life. My body felt weak, my arm sore but not the soul inside my heart, the spark within my heart is brighter than bright, for I really think I met an Angel in disguise.

Once we arrived at the station, he thanked me and gave me his blessings as he gently stretched his hand to touch my hand just like the man I'd seen in the Mexican countryside. He waved back and I felt human one more time.

I Want to Worship

In the first universal church of your being,
    kneel at your altar and pray for deliverance—

light candles and incense in your private chamber,
    open all your divine bows and buttons,

all your ethereal hooks and lace,
    murmuring earthly psalms

from your hymnal to wash your sacred feet,
    anointing your holy flesh

    with virgin oils.

Worshipping you from your own genesis.
    Worshipping your body of God.

Your holy lands awaken
    the inner congregation.

Help me to rise and open
    the sanctified door of your temple.

I'll never be interested
    in   any   other   religion.

In Memory of Uncle Manuel

Naked fury in sepia-photographed memories—
out of the rain, a man with a straw hat emerges.
The past behind his peaceful, sometimes raucous life
rests tethered in a straw armless chair.

With arms closed, he tells stories of farmworkers
sitting on boulders under mesquite trees
eating early harvest, carrots, green beans,
corn cooked over wild wood, fallen branches.

Fallen angels found on desert sand,
where blistered feet step on deadly snakes,
blistering Arizona heat, Yuma fields
dry and insipid predictability.

Harmonic junction played in unison,
after the sun ran away from the shadows chasing him,
waltzing, flying, dancing, on the vine, flower and fruit.
Stories of youth in a distant land across the line.

Back in the land where he grew up,
his rough hands built permanent monuments,
at the house where mother's love lives,
cement, brick and mortar, walls, and floors.

The whimsical honeysuckle vine midnight fragrance
pleasantly releases the memory of both—
under the fig tree, under the stars, dark leaves rustle
moonlit sky in sepia.

In the Water

I am not a swimmer, but I like feeling
weightless when I am in the pool.
A different element. Saline water, gentle water.

Floating on the surface, eyes closed,
extended arms, breath held,
I pretend to be the stick figure on the City Lights books.

No rolling, no swashing, no crashing, no movement
just floating, pretending to be lightweight.
No bones, no flesh, only the spirit in the water.

Inantzin / Madre / Mother

for Doña Elena, my Momma

One womb, two sons, three daughters
four seasons,
seventy-three sunrises,
seventy-two sunsets.
Many days of loving, teaching,
guiding.

The best cook in the world!
Along with dad, working hard at
restaurants they owned.
Dad's illness took him away first.
Mom held the sails high,
our sinking boat.

Didn't drown but kept afloat.
Destiny, cruel—
sometimes gentle.
One day, the wind changed direction,
my weathervane and compass
also changed.

Only one way out—
north, I came.
From here I remember THE ONE
whose womb like good soil gave us life.
Although the landscape is treacherous
it must be walked.

The path is long…
I raise the torch lit by the spark
Mom and Dad gave me.

Thank you both for giving me light,
thunder
and fire!

India Flashback

*Yesterday's visit to Redmond Goodwill brought back
some unexpected flashbacks, such as those from my
stay in India back in 1981–82*

Images, sounds, fragrances, smoke from crops
and burning pyres, marigolds floating on holy rivers,
solid brass gongs and cymbals, khartals, bells
and mridanga drums, Hindi, Guyarati, Urdu languages.

Where barefoot pilgrims walk around
holy sites, holy trees, holy lands.
Cows roaming through traffic,
betle nut–chew juice spat on sidewalks.
Chai vendor and the bidi-wala,
chickpea puris
and the monkey
on the server's shoulder.

Honk—honk—beep—beep—gang—bang
gang—bang—honk—honk
and PLEASE HONK! the bumper sign says
Honk—honk—honk!
The cow's crossing the road,
Have patience! You can't rush your mother.

Where humans can live humbly if they so desire.
Where austerity, abstinence, self-control are king.
Where Holy Men preach and live austerely,
fixing the universal problems in one sitting.

Brahma knows it, Shiva destroys it, Vishnu sustains it,
while the monkeys eat the alms given, chickpeas and sweets,
offerings left at the feet of holy effigies, deities.
Pilgrims of their own faith.

Sadhana: I practiced back then when I could bend and sit cross-legged for hours, meditating on Tulsi wooden beads, living the simple monastic life. I learned well,
I only use what I need,

Om Shanti

Mother's Garden

When I smell fresh-cut grass,
mother's memory comes to mind.

I can see Mom walking along
the cobblestone path below
the fig and jacaranda trees.

She airily tended to her garden,
talked to the flowers
whose ponderous voices silently
harnessed uncanny messages.

She dug her hands in damp soft soil
to plant seeds and bulbs to grow,
to blossom under the sky, rain, and sun.

Fresh-cut grass, fragrant memory
to soothe my soul.

Ode to an Old Typewriter

Last night, I dug it up from the basement.
Dad's old typewriter, as I've done before.
Although tired and lonely under fine dust,
rusted out from all the letters written before.

It was long ago when my father,
returned from the land up north,
heard of Italian typewriting machines
the invention of Camillo Olivetti.

I began to strike the key-tops, but the ribbon spool
was loose. Then the typebars jammed—
letter in deep dark black ink after the platen
and the feed roller gummed up in the grim of night.

Slowly I began to type,
familiar sound, clack, clack, clack, ding!
The light of day will see the letters fly.
I just hope the ribbon will hold,

for the ropes within each clack, clack, clack, ding!
Ring, swish and fly through the right.
The platen to the left, a new line will pour
out of dusty keys: tap, tap, tap.

Sentiment given typed, black ink on paper white,
only the typewriter knows how hard it is—
to touch the keys Dad once did
the same keys I strike, while wiping tears from my eyes.

Our Lives Suspended Until Further Notice

*as we sail through these uncertain times, we need to
live, love, and speak with care; life is beautiful*

When I think about dying,
I think about previous deaths
some tragic, some natural,
however, there isn't anything
close to dying while breathing.

The air we breathe sustains us,
we need clean air to live
to create, to love, to live, to be.
None of us chose to be exposed,
yet here we are, living in the epicenter

the zoo, dying while breathing—
breathing while dying.
Virulent baseless ideas, paranoia,
lack of understanding,
unknown germs, silent, invisible,

intangible, undetected.
World war without bullets
bombs, gases, but plain air.
Only we can save ourselves
from ourselves.

Potato Revenge

Late-afternoon cooking,
clumsy handling of the knife,
sleazy potato didn't want
to be sliced.

I believe I heard the beleaguered
zucchini, pungent onions, and carrots
laugh in unison while the pompous cauliflower
yelled from inside the cooking pot,

"We'd cook you if we could,"
while I wiped the blood away
from the knife's rippled edge
that cut through my flesh.

The vegetables had the last laugh
but I ate them anyway
with pumpernickel bread
and a sip of Chardonnay.

Remember When We Were Water?

Trümmelbach Falls, Switzerland

Pure, flowing liquid,
torrential-loaded, perfect.
Serene rain, transparent and soluble crystals,
swift as lightning in a magical stream
where all the ancient stories
dissolve…

Back then we created
our own light and reflected everything,
absolutely everything!
Splashed and dissolved,
we floated on that eternal sleep,
spinning and crashing without fear.

We twisted effortlessly,
descending between rocks and sand.
We touched every corner, soaked
every rock and pebble
dissolving into each other
without haste and still together
emanating the flow of our union,
we tasted the nectar of ecstasy
as we drowned in that spring
of pleasure, dissolved
with each other
like water.

Second Chance

*an ekphrastic poem/art exchange, 2015,
for Margaret Rozenberg*

Last night I gazed at the sky—
stared beyond the stars.

Earlier, I saw the sun bulging
beyond the horizon
pushing the darkness

as if giving the universe
a second chance.

Beyond the bird feeder, goldfinches zoom away
towards the white shirts
hanging on the long clothesline.

I run outdoors,
beyond the knoll and the cellars

amidst the sleeping daffodils
the wimpy crocuses terrified—
a bad windstorm looming…

Tonight, I stand still—
look beyond the frame to see the sun
pushing the sky away!

The Man on the Exit Ramp

On a dark rainy Sunday night, neon lights make raindrops glitter & shine. I saw the man with the long coat walking on two aluminum legs. Holding a sitting stool in one hand, a walking cane in the other. He swayed as he walked. His scarf was swinging from left to right. When the light turned, he walked across 8th Ave. South to sit by the corner light, and wait, and wait until kindness dropped in his can. I turned the corner, and I turned my mind inward to see if I would have the guts to live regardless of the circumstances. The image of fortitude and honest determination provided by the man walking on two aluminum legs to work the ramp at I-5 below the sign that reads "Seattle, Jesus Loves You" haunts me.

Travelling by Whale

inspired by Mauricio Robalino's painting, c. 2022

Killer Whale swam across the bay
Nanasimgat's wife sat behind his dorsal fin
She talked to the otters
Warning them about the hunters.
Raven Guide used
his seductive charming voice,
a lovely bell-like croon,
one of the most beautiful sounds
in the world,
to lead them to safety.

Two Palm Trees

When I think of you,
always by my side,
I can't decide which
songs the breeze
will make you sing,

or murmur
between the leaves
of your branches.

The burning sun
and the breezy air,
tickles my side,
but the evening breeze
brings your softer, smoother touch

and your serenade
echoes the sound of low tide's
ebb and flow,

always by your side.

Vanished

In the dark of night, evil grows.
Confusion tendrils, creeps up
intimidating immigrant folk.
Signed releases on command
not knowing it was a trap, a lie
by the Deceitful States of America.
Innocent young men sent
to Salvadorean jails.

Hate is the motive, revenge is the aim,
removal is the goal.
The Constitution twisted like Gumby,
someone, please tell the Lady of the Harbor
her torch has been off
since November 5th, 2024,
Election Day, doomsday
for the America we knew.

What Work Is

after Philip Levine

I know what work is
work is what I do
eight hours
away from home
work is the place
where I contribute
and get paid
where I repair machines
work is what I do with them.

At work I hear a festival
of languages
I call work the United Nations
under one roof
work is rewarding
when I succeed
when I beat the odds
implausible possibilities
I use my brain to do my work.

I go to work even though
I do not feel like going to work
after work I read poems
old ones new ones
Keats   Byron   Levine   Oliver
Espada   Borges   Kozer
that's what I like about work
because it helps me
with *my* work.

Why Poetry?

because:

Poetry is the key that opens minds and hearts
Poetry is father and daughter reading together
Poetry is the sound of water
Poetry is the gentle movement of the blue herons
Poetry is the color of flowers
Poetry is the feel of the cold wind and rain
Poetry is the sun slowly rising
Poetry is the distant sound of birds
Poetry is the clarity of water
Poetry is a gentle smile behind the mask
Poetry is the glorious color of tulips
Poetry is the joyous laughter of children
Poetry is the shelter of our worries
Poetry is the answer to our doubts
Poetry is proof of our existence
Poetry is the healing balm for the soul
Poetry brings people together
Poetry is light
Poetry is life!

Notes

"Borinquen"

"tierra santa, tierra pura" is from the Los Lobos song "Maricela" from *Colossal Head* (1996).

Last stanza: Andrés Jiménez, *En Vivo* (Cuarto Menguante Records, 2006)

"Daffodils and Dandelions"

In traditional Chinese and Native American medicine, dandelion root has long been used to treat stomach and liver conditions. Herbalists today believe that it can aid in the treatment of many ailments, including acne, eczema, high cholesterol, heartburn, gastrointestinal disorders, diabetes, and even cancer.

"By the line of the spine"

History, war, military, battles, native Americans, and the amazing discovery of *Black Hawk*, or as the original title of the book reads: *Life of Ma-ka-tai-me-she-kia-kiak, or Black Hawk*, dictated by himself. Written by J. B. Patterson. This book and others alike cannot be borrowed. So, if you're curious, you have to go see the book in person at the Seattle Central Public Library.

Acknowledgments

The author wishes to thank and acknowledge the previous journals and venues where several poems in this collection previously appeared, sometimes in earlier versions.

Brightly Press: "Today I Killed a Spider" and "Visit to Dachau"

City of Shoreline Cultural and Community Services Public Art and online project: "Ode to an Oak Tree," "Oda a un roble viejo", "Greensward," "Césped"

Footbridge Above the Falls: "Monk's Dream on Monet's Nymphéas bleus" and "Only a Dream"

Gazoobitales.com: "MEX- I - CAN"

La Bloga: "Brown Angels at Work," "In Praise of Poets Responding to SB 1070," "Minimum Wage," "Wind"

Latino Northwest Magazine: Speaking Desde Las Heridas: "MEX- I - CAN"

Lowriting: Shots, Rides & Stories from the Chicano Soul: "Reminiscing"

Pirene's Fountain Vol. 6, Issue 14 (2013): "Smoke"

Puro Chicanx Writers of the 21st Century: "Show Me Your Papers"

Here, There, and Everywhere: Redmond Association of Spokenword Poetry Anthology: "Smoke"

Revolution and Reclamation: "We Danced"

Subprimal Poetry Art/Music, Issue 1:"Mexica Tiahui"

The Sylvan Echo: "Gravity"

Viva la Word Anthology: "Colors of Life"

Yellow Medicine Review: "Daffodils and Dandelions," "Guatemalan Miracle," "Washing the Dishes," "Whisper"

Some poems in this collection also appeared in prior collections:

All Our Brown-Skinned Angels (MoonPath Press, 2012)

When There Were No Borders (Flower Song Press, 2021)

Gratitude

I am grateful first and foremost to Lana Hechtman Ayers for publishing my new work fourteen years since the release of my first collection, *All Our Brown-Skinned Angels*. The title poem from that collection inspired an acoustic interpretation by Gretchen Yanover, a Seattle composer and cellist, appearing on her fifth CD, *Holding / Movement*, Track 7, titled "If brown angels could fly." I am very honored and grateful for her collaboration. This collection shows more of the being inside this brown body as I continue learning, mentoring, translating, writing, and sharing poetry with the public.

Much appreciation to the World Enough Writers team for all the magic, ingenuity, and skillful details on the elaboration of this book, especially Tonya Namura for her excellent book design.

Gratitude to my wife for catching my errors, tolerating my anxiety when I am not holding pen and paper, and for being my first reader.

I am immensely happy to be able to use one of the late Alfredo Arreguín's (1935–2023) works, titled *Sedona*, courtesy of the Rob Schouten Gallery and Sculpture Garden in Langley, Washington. A very big *Thank You* to Rob and Victory Schouten. Alfredo was a man of Color and Words; he painted his poems on the canvas, and his work lends itself to a poetic rendition.

I am grateful to the following people for helping me become a better person and writer: Lorna Dee Cervantes, John Burgess, Griffith Williams, Francisco X. Alarcón, Liz Barry, Joan Rabinowitz, Levi Fuller, Christopher J. Jarmick, David Post, Ghaddra González Castillo, Becca

Lavin, Leopoldo Seguel, Richard Gold, Nicole Renée La Follette, John Martinez, Mary Ellen Talley, Ellen Ziegler, Rachel Androski, Shaun McMichael, Emily Shallman, Neil Scott, Douglas Cole, Gus Denhart, Abel Salas, Tony Gomez, Paula Madrigal, and Teo Benson—"The Free-Range Poets at the Meadowbrook Pond," and many more wonderful humans.

About the Artist

ALFREDO ARREGUÍN (1935–2023)*

Alfredo Arreguín was a very driven and inspired artist and he painted up until three weeks before his passing. His work was exhibited for six years running at the Rob Schouten Gallery on Whidbey Island, Washington, where he was featured in four solo exhibitions of his work, two of which while he was still alive.

Arreguín's vibrant patterned work was inspired by his love of animals, his Mexican heritage, and his admiration of Frida Kahlo and others.

Arreguín came to Seattle from Morelia, Michoacán, Mexico in 1956. After completing his studies at the University of Washington in 1969 he became a seminal artist in the Seattle art world, opening doors for many Hispanic and Latino artists. His work is featured in the Smithsonian Museum of American Art as well as the Seattle Art Museum and numerous other museums.

*Artist information is courtesy of the Rob Schouten Gallery and Sculpture Garden, Langley, Washington, https://www.robschoutengallery.com/

About the Author

Raúl Sánchez is a self-taught poet whose work reflects the immigrant experience as well as his own story. He volunteers as a bilingual mentor in middle schools, detention centers, housing for the homeless and disabled, as well as with immigrants and laborers. He leads community "Poetry in the Park" readings May–September in northeast Seattle. During COVID, he installed a "Poetry Box" in front of his home filled with single poems for the neighbors to put in their pockets as encouragement. He wrote the libretto for the Sinfonía "Moctezuma" monologue in response to Vivaldi's *Motezuma*, original version for Orquesta Northwest. Some of his poems have become permanent public art in Seattle and Shoreline.

www.ingramcontent.com/pod-product-compliance
Lightning Source LLC
Chambersburg PA
CBHW030526080526
44586CB00011B/336